Governor Zell Miller's
Reading Initiative

FREDERIC REMINGTON

FREDERIC
REMINGTON
ELIZABETH VAN STEENWYK

Franklin Watts
New York / Chicago / London /Toronto / Sydney
A First Book

Library of Congress Cataloging-in-Publication Data

Van Steenwyk, Elizabeth.
Frederic Remington / by Elizabeth Van Steenwyk.
p. cm. — (A First Book)
Includes bibliographical references and index.
ISBN 0-531-20172-4
1. Remington, Frederic, 1861–1909—Juvenile literature.
2. Artists—United States—Biography—Juvenile literature.
[1. Remington, Frederic, 1861–1909. 2. Artists.] I. Title. II. Series.
N6537.R4V33   1994
709'.2—dc20   94-2240
[B]   CIP AC

CONTENTS

FREDERIC REMINGTON

Self Portrait on a Horse *was painted in oil on canvas by Remington in 1890.*

INTRODUCTION

Frederic Sackrider Remington was a turn-of-the-century American artist whose art documented one of the most dramatic stories of our time—the settling of the West. His artistic vision continues to be felt today in movies, stories, and songs.

Remington's career lasted only twenty-four years until his early death at the age of forty-eight. He left, however, a large and distinguished legacy of more than three thousand illustrations and paintings, twenty-two sculptures, and more than one hundred literary and journalistic pieces.

Artists who came before Remington illustrated the western scene and others followed him to do the same. But none did as well or as realistically, for he painted and sketched each subject without prejudice as he saw it. Only toward the end of his life did he begin to paint in the new Impressionist style.

Remington said, "I knew the West better than any other man." His work echoes his words.

1 AN UNDISCIPLINED BEGINNING

When Frederic Remington was nineteen years old, he traveled to the western part of the United States for the first time. It was a trip that shaped his life and career. He said, ". . . the more I looked the more the panorama unfolded." Then he went on to tell of the movement and shape and color of the countryside. His young artist's eye detailed and remembered everything. The West would become the focus of his life's work.

Probably the most startling thing he saw on that trip in August 1881 was the slaughter of the buffalo in Wyoming and Montana. For generations, American Indians killed them only as needed for their food supply, but more than five thousand white hunters had moved in to shoot them for their skins. At the end of the summer more than one million buffalo had been slaughtered. It probably explained "the heavy feel in the atmosphere" that Remington never forgot.

*An engraving of the buffalo slaughter in the
West made from a Remington drawing*

During his lifetime he turned again and again to paint and sketch the drama of the American West. His art left a legacy of impressions from that period in history that lives on today in movies, books, and songs.

The American Civil War had been raging for nearly six months when Frederic Sackrider Remington was born on October 4, 1861, in Canton, New York. His father owned and edited the *Plain Dealer*, a successful newspaper in town. He served as postmaster as well, appointed by the new Lincoln administration in Washington, D.C.

Mr. Remington was a tall, slender man who made his living from his knowledge of language and was considered a great storyteller among his many friends. He was also a man of action. Eight weeks after the birth of Frederic, he enlisted in Company D of Scott's 900, the Eleventh New York Cavalry, and rode off to war, eventually leading the company in skirmishes and engagements.

Mr. Remington returned home in 1865 at the war's end with the rank of colonel and a reputation for having been a fearless, brave soldier. He resumed editorship of the *Plain-Dealer* and once again became a leader of the community.

As the only child of this prominent ex-soldier and of a retiring, artistic mother, Frederic developed

Top: *Grandmother Remington's house on Court Street, Canton, New York, where Frederic Remington was born on October 4, 1861*

Left: *Remington at age four with his mother, Clara Bascomb Sackrider Remington, a shy woman but strong in convictions*

into a hyperactive, spoiled, overweight terror. Although he occasionally spent time quietly drawing on his slate, often he was leading a lively pack of boys into mischief. In the summer, he loved to swim in the wide, dangerous Grasse River although he was forbidden to do so by his mother.

Young Frederic paid small attention to school lessons, preferring to play "cowboys and Indians" and teasing the neighbor girls. Not only did children he bothered dislike him, their parents called him disagreeable and dreadful. He once ruined a girl's doll by dousing it with water. Another time, he caught a playmate's cat and painted it green.

In the summer of 1869, half the town's business area was destroyed by fire, including the Remington newspaper offices. A month later, an official fire department was established, with Mr. Remington as assistant engineer. He arranged to have Frederic become the mascot for Engine Company One, hoping to corral the boy's instinct for mischief. Frederic soon had his own uniform, which he wore when he marched with the department in parades.

One year later, a second fire destroyed the *Plain-Dealer*'s new offices. Colonel Remington looked for different work and became Collector of U.S. Customs in nearby Ogdensburg. Young

Engine Number One personnel of Canton fire department with ten-year-old Remington as its mascot

Frederic, now called Puffy because of his size, became the leader of a new pack of boys in Ogdensburg. He invented games for them to play and drew sketches, mostly of horses, to amuse them. He enjoyed a happy-go-lucky, undisciplined life. Although mischievous, Frederic always had a strong sense of security because he knew how much his parents loved him.

In 1875, Frederic was ready to enter high school but there was none in Ogdensburg. His parents decided he would attend Vermont Episcopal Institute (VEI), which was conducted with strict military discipline. The Colonel may have hoped his son would benefit from the cadet life or possibly choose a military career.

Frederic was eager for the experience at first, but soon changed his mind. Although he received his first formal art lessons at VEI, he hated the rest of it, especially military drill. The following year he transferred to Highland Military Academy. Again a halfhearted student, he was popular among his classmates for drawing amusing caricatures of teachers and officers. He drew bold figures, many of them in motion, but with little proportion or sensitivity. By the following year, his drawings were as much a part of his letters and lessons as his words were. Although his personality remained playful and lighthearted, his serious side began to emerge as he worried about his father's failing health.

In June 1878, he completed his schoolwork at Highland, and that fall, entered the Yale School of Fine Arts. It was not a popular decision with his parents or their families. Most of his aunts and uncles thought of art as something that women dabbled in while awaiting marriage. Further, no

Right: *Remington accompanied Nelson A. Miles on several expeditions and made this pencil sketch of him in 1878. The artist would have been aware of Miles and other Civil War military leaders from his student days at Highland Military Academy.*

GEN. N.A. MILES.

Bottom: *Remington was the only male in his class at the Yale School of Fine Arts when he began in 1878. His classroom was in the basement.*

one in the family really thought that Frederic had talent. But his parents continued to be lenient and allowed their only child to do as he pleased.

Frederic was the only young man in his class and worked alone in a basement room, copying casts of antique sculpture. He found still-life drawing a bore, but his first cartoon to appear in the student newspaper brought him a feeling of satisfaction.

When he returned for a second year, he was again the only man in class. Courses in perspective, anatomy, color, and composition had become even more boring and he did not apply himself. But after he tried out for football and was accepted because of his size (at 5 feet, 9 inches [1.75 m] tall, he weighed 190 pounds [86 kg]) college life became brighter. The Yale team of 1878 was considered the best in the country, and Frederic remained proud of his association with it for the rest of his life. One of his professors remarked, however, that the often bruised and battered Remington was one of the most unusual-looking art students he'd ever had.

At home for Christmas vacation, Frederic found his father seriously ill with tuberculosis. Despite the best care then available, the Colonel died in mid-February. Frederic never returned to Yale. He felt adrift, not knowing what to do with his life and

Right: On November 2, 1878, the student newspaper, the Yale Courant, *printed Remington's first published illustration, which brought him welcomed attention from other students.*

Bottom: Called "the best in the country," the Yale football team counted Remington as one of its own. He is shown third from the right, top row.

COLLEGE RIFF-RAFF.

IV.

"Good gracious, old fellow, what have you been doing with yourself?"

Rusher on the University foot ball team:—"Oh! nothing in particular; a fellow must get used to these Rugby rules, you know.—The doctor says I'll be all right by Thanksgiving, and that's all I care for now."

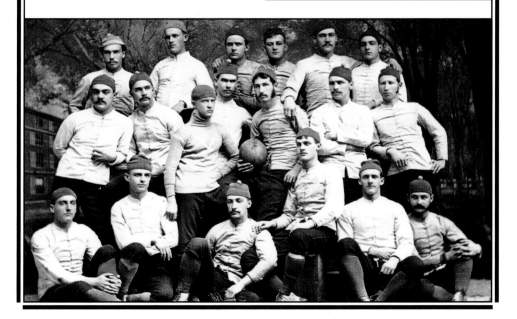

lacking the discipline to take charge of it. His uncles, who now looked after financial matters for him and his mother, decided that the young Remington should become a businessman and forget all thoughts of becoming an artist.

Remington moved to Albany to be near his Uncle Mart, who took charge of finding him work. Soon Frederic became a clerk in the governor's office, a job for which he was not qualified, and soon quit. Uncle Mart then found him a job on a newspaper. This, too, Frederic quit after a few months.

After several more attempts at employment, he returned to Canton, where his mother now lived, and recklessly spent the first installment of his inheritance. During all this time, he had occasionally sketched, but without any serious effort or direction.

After one more failed attempt at finding him work, the family seemed to give up, and the summer of 1881 found Frederic out of work and without any plan for his future. It didn't concern him. Frederic Remington decided it was time for a vacation from all the boredom of his life and headed west.

2

IN SEARCH OF THE FUTURE

When Frederic Remington traveled west for a holiday in 1881, he hoped the road might also lead to a fortune. Like nearly everyone else who headed west during these years of exploration and settlement, he dreamed of bettering himself. First, the trappers and traders came to collect lush animal pelts and hides to sell back east. Next came a great rush of miners who pounded and sluiced the earth, looking for the glitter of gold and silver. Not long after, cattlemen arrived, searching for fertile fields and valleys on which to fatten their herds.

In the years before Remington's first visit in 1881, the Sioux, Cheyenne, Arapaho, and other Plains tribes increasingly resisted the numbers of whites moving onto their land. American Indians challenged the U.S. Army many times, achieving their most famous victory at the Little Bighorn River in Montana. There, on June 25, 1876, the Sioux fought and killed General George Armstrong

HARPER'S WEEKLY.
JOURNAL OF CIVILIZATION.

Vol. XXIX—No. 1473.

NEW YORK, SATURDAY, MARCH 28, 1885.

Ejecting an Oklahoma Boomer, *Remington's second published work, redrawn by a* Harper's Weekly *engraver as was the custom. It was based on Remington's experience when he traveled into Indian Territory from his sheep ranch near Peabody, Kansas, in 1883.*

Custer and his men. The Army continued to pressure the Indians, however, and forced many onto reservations.

Now, with his artist's eye, Remington came and observed the remnants of tribes who refused to settle behind fences. He also watched the cavalrymen guiding settlers to and from the safety of forts. He listened to cowboys and ranch hands spin their tales of life on the western plains.

Then, on a piece of wrapping paper, Remington sketched a scene of the West and sent it off to *Harper's Weekly* magazine in New York. Although his technique remained undisciplined, Remington's sketch was recognized as totally authentic to the western scene, and the art director accepted it immediately.

Remington felt encouraged by this small success, but it wasn't a living. He returned home and went back to a clerical job. Unmotivated, he spent most of his time sketching other workers. The following year, he celebrated his twenty-first birthday and received the rest of his inheritance. He quit his job and turned his attention west once again.

He had stayed in touch with a former classmate who settled in Kansas on a sheep ranch. Remington's imagination pushed him to buy a similar ranch, sight unseen, near his friend's; and once again, he left New York and headed west.

Kansas lacked the sagebrush beauty of Montana. In fact, early Kansas had little to offer but dust in the summer and mud in the winter. Remington's three-room ranch house near Peabody, Kansas, contained none of the comforts of his eastern life, and worse, the sheep he'd just bought were dirty, smelly creatures.

It was not a good beginning, but Frederic had come for the adventure and quickly adapted to Western dress and attitude. Now weighing 220 pounds (100 kg), he soon gained the attention of the locals as he galloped on a little pony named Terra-Cotta through the streets of town, waving his sombrero.

Although he invested his entire inheritance in the ranch, he left its direction to others and left it altogether if there was something else to do. He loved competing with idle ranch hands in boxing, bronco riding, steer wrestling, and chasing rabbits. Meanwhile, he continued to sketch and draw on whatever paper he could find. He was becoming better at observing, then sketching in bold, clean lines, although his sense of proportion remained poor and inaccurate.

By now the locals resented his carefree approach to ranching. They had to work hard. He seemed not to work at all. On Halloween, he put the preacher's buggy with a cow inside it on top of the church. This only reaffirmed his neighbors' attitude that he was an eastern playboy who lacked the discipline to accomplish anything serious in life.

After another prank that could have resulted in serious damage, Remington left town. He had decided to dispose of his ranch by this time anyway, and auctioned off everything in February 1884. He had not become rich but did recoup most of his investment. When the new owner moved in, he found Remington's sketches covering many of the walls of the ranch buildings and painted them out.

Remington settled in Kansas City, Missouri, to try the hardware business with a partner. This, too, was an unsuccessful choice and he found himself adrift once again. More and more he turned to sketching, and one friend claimed "he could draw a picture of a bucking pony that was livelier than the original."

He still had money to invest and decided to become a silent partner in a saloon. He soon had enough income to buy a small home and felt it was time to propose marriage to a young woman named Eva Caten. They had met at a neighbor's home in Canton some years before and had an understanding that they would marry one day. After the ceremony on October 1, 1884, Remington brought his bride home to Kansas City.

It was not what she had expected. The prairie town of 75,000 was the livestock center of the country. Cattle broke free on their way to the stockyards and turned the streets into smelly quagmires. Cowboys, gamblers, and outlaws roamed in search of excitement and usually found it. Even worse, the

Left: *Photograph of the artist. He described himself as having "a warm, blond English complexion and light hair."*

Right: *From his first year as a commercial artist, Remington's income permitted his young wife, Eva Adele Caten Remington, to dress in a stylish manner she enjoyed.*

new Mrs. Remington didn't know her husband owned a saloon. She did not approve of saloons, much less their owners. Despite the sketches he brought home to her each day, she remained upset and disapproving. She returned to New York for the holidays and did not come back.

In his loneliness, Remington turned more and more to his art, now beginning to paint in both oil and watercolor. Three of his paintings were displayed in an art store and quickly sold. When another customer wanted him to duplicate one of his pictures, the art store owner told Remington, "Never duplicate anything. Keep conceiving new pictures." It was advice the artist would follow all of his life.

Encouraged, he submitted more sketches to *Harper's Weekly*, which were accepted. Now he began to feel that he could earn a living with his art. It was the only thing he really wanted to do. Besides, nothing else seemed to work for him, not even the saloon business.

He returned east to his wife, settling in Brooklyn, not far from the New York publishers he hoped soon would be clamoring for his art. But his mind and eyes and heart remained full of the West. The western scene was waiting to be immortalized on canvas by Frederic Remington.

3 THE COWBOY GOES TO BROOKLYN

The year 1885 was a perfect time for Frederic Remington to begin his professional art career. In October, the country's attention was focused out west; in particular on the Apache chief Geronimo. He had emerged as a leader when the government began to resettle American Indians to other parts of the country. Now readers in the East clamored to know more about him.

Henry Harper, one of the most powerful publishers in New York, bought two Remington sketches immediately, saying his work had the "ring of new and live material." In fact, Remington's drawings were so realistic they soon would end the Victorian, or romantic, era in illustration.

The following June, Harper sent the young artist to New Mexico "in serch [sic] of Geronimo." While on this trip, Remington began a journal. His writing career flourished along with his art, as he began to publish articles to accompany his sketches.

Although Remington was commissioned by Harper's Weekly to cover the search for Geronimo, the American Apache shown here in about 1895, the artist's participation was brief.

Although Remington briefly investigated the Army's plans to hunt down Geronimo, he quickly concluded he did not want to be a part of this expedition and changed the focus of his trip to soldiering in the Southwest. He began to photograph soldiers at work. Using photos and quick pencil sketches with notation on color, he drew them with complete accuracy.

In particular, his drawings of horses were realistic enough to change the art world's concept of them. Remington's innovation was helped by Eadweard Muybridge, who had taken sequence photography of horses in action, proving Remington's interpretation. Prior to Remington, horses had been drawn in a static, or hobbyhorse, position. In these drawings, the front legs extended forward and the back legs extended backward. But Remington knew the animals well. He had read about them and sketched them constantly as he was growing up, ridden horses all his life, and studied their anatomy in classes at Yale. Now he drew them realistically in action. To show a gallop, he sketched them with forelegs tucked in a leap and back legs off the ground. Viewers and critics praised what he'd done, and he was later credited as being the first American artist to give character to the horse in art.

A Dash for the Timber, *an oil on canvas,*
was commissioned by Edmund Converse.
It was completed in 1889.

In 1887, Remington had a backlog of commissions and he worked seven days a week to complete them. As his reputation grew, better engravers were assigned to him by his publishers. In those early days of publishing, all sketches were copied onto wood blocks to be printed. As artists became better known, they were given better engravers to transfer their work.

In the fall, Remington was asked to illustrate a book called *Ranch Life and the Hunting Trail* by its author, Theodore Roosevelt. The two men were alike in many ways. They were easterners who loved the West, pursued adventure and the outdoor life, then published their experiences. Although Remington and the future president of the United States disliked each other at first, Remington was challenged by the opportunity to illustrate his book.

Remington's life now fell into a pattern. Publishers sent him on trips to the West where he sketched and visited soldiers, cowboys, and Indians, then returned home to paint and write of his experiences. Usually he left on the trips overweight and out of shape for the grueling physical challenges. He was a perfect candidate for teasing by the soldiers, to test his endurance and sense of humor. When he rode with the Buffalo Soldiers, a nickname given to the all-black Tenth United States Cavalry, a rattlesnake in his bedding and rocks

Top: *Section of typical engraving room showing die cutters, plate engravers, pentographers, sketchmakers, and hand engravers at work. It is here that the designs are put on copper rollers by means of pressure, cutting, or etching.*

Right: The Apache War: Indian Scouts on Geronimo's Trail *in* Harper's Weekly, *January 9, 1886, was Remington's first professional appearance.*

beneath his sleeping pad mysteriously appeared. They were taken in stride and without complaint by Remington. Before he returned home, he was elected an honorary member of the Cavalry and he was 20 pounds (9 kg) thinner.

Despite Remington's success as a magazine illustrator, he felt ready to move on with his career. His talent had been growing, maturing beyond the pen-and-ink sketches and the black-and-white washes he presently sold to magazines. For some time he had worked privately in watercolors, exhibited his paintings, and even sold a few of them. His awareness of color was constant. In his articles, he spoke of the "golden light" of the canyon wall, the "gray tints" of camp, and sunsets too beautiful to capture with the artist's brush.

He began to work in oils now and completed a large painting of a western scene in time to have it submitted to the 1889 Paris International Exposition. He then traveled to Mexico on another sponsored trip. When he returned with many ideas for sketches and articles, he learned that he had won a second-class medal at the Paris Exposition. It was a great honor, for it meant that western subjects painted realistically finally had been recognized in the best art circles in the world.

Now he was asked to create four hundred illustrations for Longfellow's poem *Hiawatha*, to be

The Ambushed Picket *appeared as an illustration in* Harper's Weekly *on June 8, 1889, although the idea for it had taken shape several years earlier. This watercolor, pencil, pen, and ink drawing on paper was probably produced shortly after the 1886 trip in search of Geronimo.*

reprinted in book form. This project kept him busy throughout most of the summer in 1890, but the generous fee he received allowed him and his wife to build a beautiful home in New Rochelle, New York. After much thought, he named his new home Endion, which, in the Ojibwa language means "the place where I live."

Traveling to Montana and South Dakota in the fall, he foresaw a major battle looming between the

Plains Indians and the U.S. government. As he wrote a friend, "There's going to be a major row," and he wanted to be on hand to record it. He felt the coming conflict had been provoked by the government. It had replaced experienced Indian agents with inexperienced political appointees to handle serious problems in relocating the Indians. Remington wrote in an article: "Let us preserve the native American race, which is following the buffalo into painted pictures and printed books."

In 1890, Remington and his wife bought a house in New Rochelle, New York, which they named Endion. In the Ojibwa language, the word means "the place where I live."

He returned home briefly, then traveled again to South Dakota, riding with Army lieutenant Edward Casey and a band of Cheyenne Indian scouts. On December 30, Remington rode with a smaller group going to the Pine Ridge Indian Agency. Halfway there, they realized something serious had happened as they met Sioux in war paint who were behaving in a hostile manner. Warned by one of their scouts that the Sioux "hearts were bad," they returned to Lieutenant Casey's camp.

There, they learned that one day earlier, on December 29, a massacre had occurred. Nearly three hundred Sioux men, women, and children had been killed by the Seventh United States Cavalry at Wounded Knee Creek, not far from the agency. It was the last armed conflict between the Army and the Indians as the latter reluctantly moved to reservations.

Remington rode to the camp of the Seventh Cavalry a week later and collected stories from the soldiers to include in his article for *Harper's Weekly*. Although he sometimes expressed prejudice toward minorities in personal letters, Remington never displayed anything but the truth in his art.

An era in American history was ending. Buffalo, which once roamed the prairies, had disappeared. The American Indians, who had depended on the buffalo for food and shelter and clothing,

Remington sketched A Cheyenne Camp *in 1888 to illustrate an article for* Century *magazine about his experiences visiting the encampment of Chief Whirlwind.*

now depended on the government. Much of the land that once belonged to Indians now had been settled by white farmers. Stretching across the prairie, barren grasslands had become fertile farms, causing the director of the census to say at the close of 1890, "There can hardly be said to be a frontier line" in the United States.

The era of the western frontier had passed, but not the public's desire to know and remember it. Frederic Remington's name was fast becoming a part of the western history he sought to preserve through his art.

4

EVOLUTION OF THE ARTIST

Henry Harper, the publisher, began a publicity campaign in his weekly and monthly publications to call attention to Remington's art. Remington also felt the time had come for creating new interest in his work since he was looking for new subjects to paint. After several trips to Mexico, he began to paint and draw scenes of outdoor life there.

In June 1891, his career received even more publicity when he was elected an associate of the National Academy of Design, just one step away from the Academy's highest honor. This was a rare achievement for an artist who was only twenty-nine years old and had been illustrating for only six years and exhibiting with the Academy for five. Now he felt he needed to find even more subjects for his brush and pen and looked to Europe for them.

He made plans to go with Poultney Bigelow, a friend from Yale days. He was now a foreign corre-

Cavalryman of the Line. *Remington journeyed to Mexico in 1889 to gather material for an article about the Mexican army.*

spondent and had been assigned by a magazine to cover a pending war between Germany and Russia. Because Bigelow needed an illustrator, it was only natural that he ask his old friend from school. Remington was pleased to go with him, although he didn't know that Bigelow had a secret assignment, to spy on Russia for Germany.

Once they arrived in St. Petersburg, Bigelow disappeared for three days without telling Remington where he was going or why. The artist lost all interest in sketching as he worried and waited for his friend. During this time, he wrote home: "I have been as lonesome as a toad in a well." Once Bigelow returned and his spying activities were discovered, the Russian government asked them to leave immediately. Remington was happy to comply.

Back in the United States, Remington returned to his favorite subject, the American West. He made several quick trips to sketch trail scenes and interview cowboys, to make up the time and money lost on the Russian trip. Although he was surprised to find his sketches of the West remained popular, he still felt that their popularity couldn't last and that he needed new subjects to paint.

Again, his friend Poultney Bigelow provided an opportunity by suggesting that Remington go with him to North Africa. The artist accepted immediately

Poultney Bigelow, classmate of Remington at Yale and lifelong friend. Bigelow and Remington shared adventures in Germany and North Africa when Bigelow was a foreign correspondent and needed Remington to illustrate his newspaper articles.

and sailed off to sketch French soldiers instead of American ones. The friends had a rollicking time but, again, this was not a profitable trip for Remington. The highlight of the trip was his detailed study of Arabian horses, native to North Africa. He also lost some weight, telling the folks back home that he was now down to 210 pounds (95 kg).

In 1893, as President Grover Cleveland was reelected (although not to a consecutive term), a financial panic hit the country. Banks failed, companies went bankrupt, and much unemployment resulted. Low wages and long hours prevailed everywhere. Even Remington struggled to find assignments in the depression.

Henry Harper had discovered Owen Wister, a writer whose western stories reignited the public's interest in the West. Now Harper teamed Remington's talent to Wister's. Although Remington expressed dissatisfaction with illustrating someone else's words, he was pleased to be working. He even helped Wister by pointing out mistakes in his text. Remington, at the age of thirty-two, was an authority on western lore.

In May 1894, the Pullman Palace Car Company in Chicago cut employees' wages without lowering their rents in company housing, and the employees went on strike. In addition, Eugene V. Debs, a well-known Labor Party leader, led the American Railway Union in a boycott of the Pullman Company's cars, tying up railroad transportation nationally. Finally, President Cleveland called in federal troops to restore order.

Remington traveled to Chicago to be with the troops, whom he knew well from his days out west. He also was assigned to write and sketch the story for *Harper's*. His wife wrote to a friend that he was "always happy with the troops."

Later that year, Remington persuaded Owen Wister to join him in documenting the origins of the American cowboy. Although Wister wrote the article, Remington supplied most of the facts and illustrated it. Called "The Evolution of the Cowboy," it was published in September 1895 in *Harper's Monthly*. From it came the model of the cowboy that has been portrayed again and again in twentieth-century books and movies about the Old West, influencing the world's image of this typical American character.

Once the evolution piece was published, Remington was restless to move on to something else. One day, a visitor to his studio at Endion watched how quickly Remington worked. Impressed, he said, "You're not an illustrator so much as you're a sculptor."

Excited by this idea, Remington asked a sculptor about technique. He was told, "Forget technique and it will take care of itself."

He worked quickly and confidently in plasticine, a commercial wax, on the figure of a cowboy astride a horse, or bronco, as Remington called the animal. By the end of summer, he had finished it and sent the model off to be cast in bronze.

The public was eager to see what Remington had done in this new (to him) art form. *Harper's*

The Puncher. *Remington painted this oil on canvas in 1895 at the end of the frontier period in American history. Paintings like this helped to perpetuate the concept of the American cowboy in frontier history.*

Weekly carried a full-page photograph of the piece now called *The Broncho Buster*, as well as an article by a well-known critic, Arthur Hoeber, who said, "Mr. Remington has handled his clay in a masterly way." Remington was more to the point when he wrote: "I have always had a feeling for mud." Most critics and all of the art world agreed that Remington's first sculpture was a masterpiece. He didn't disagree.

Now called the busiest artist in the world by *Harper's*, he yearned for even more fields to conquer. Military subjects were his favorites to illustrate, and he longed to be a foreign correspondent as well. "I think I smell war in the air," he told a friend as he followed the problems between Spain and Cuba.

He soon found a way to go to Cuba, as the illustrator for William Randolph Hearst, publisher of the *New York Journal*. He was teamed with Richard Harding Davis, and it was their goal to meet General Gomez, the leader of the Cuban rebels. Although they searched Cuba, they couldn't find him. Because there was no other action, Remington cabled Hearst that he wanted to return home. Hearst is said to have cabled back: "You furnish the pictures, I'll furnish the war." Remington went home anyway.

The next year and a half found Remington slowing his painting and sculpting efforts but

The Bronco Buster *was originally spelled Broncho Buster by Remington, but the patent attorney corrected the spelling when the bronze sculpture, Remington's first, was copyrighted in October 1895.*

increasing his writing output. Naturally, his subject was the West, and he seemed to write about it better than anyone else at the time. After reading one of Remington's short stories in *Harper's*, Theodore Roosevelt, who by now had become a close friend, wrote to him saying: "You are one of the men who tend to keep alive my hope in America."

In 1898, war correspondents Remington, Caspar Whitney, Grover Flint, Richard Harding Davis, and Captain Arthur H. Lee, wait at the Tampa Hotel, Tampa, Florida, to board a ship and sail to Cuba to report on the Spanish-American War.

The problem in Cuba was not going away, however, even as President William McKinley tried to intercede. He also hoped to protect Americans living in Cuba by sending the battleship *Maine* to Havana Harbor. It didn't take long for things to happen. On February 15, 1898, the *Maine* mysteriously blew up in the harbor. In April, Remington got the war he'd been waiting for.

5 THE WEST BELONGS TO HIM

Although the United States declared war on Spain on April 25, 1898, action was slow to begin. Finally, on June 14, after several false starts, troopships sailed to Cuba. Remington was on one of the first to go.

During the waiting period, Remington had not been idle. He spent time with the troops gathering in Florida and sketched and wrote articles for the newspapers he represented. He also sailed with the Navy on a blockade attempt of Cuba. His first story written on board, however, was not about a thrilling naval encounter but about the rescue of the ship's mascot, a black cat, who had fallen overboard.

Remington attached himself to the "Galloping Sixth" Cavalry as American troops began the invasion of Cuba. Although he was overweight and out of shape, Remington at first was able to keep the pace. With the soldiers, he hacked his way through dense jungle and ate and slept in driving rains and torrid temperatures. Along the way, he met his old friends, the Buffalo Soldiers of the Tenth Cavalry, and reported on their progress.

It was his friend Theodore Roosevelt, however, who provided Remington and the rest of the reporters with the most exciting stories. Roosevelt had resigned his position as assistant secretary of the Navy to organize the First U.S. Volunteer Cavalry, soon nicknamed the Rough Riders. They arrived in Cuba, eager for action.

By the end of the month, Remington began to feel the effects of the rugged outdoor life. Despite having become ill with a fever, he followed Roosevelt's unit as it advanced on Spanish soldiers. But the war Remington had been waiting for was not what he experienced. Bullets whizzed past his head, and the sight of young men wounded and dying all around him, especially those he knew personally, convinced him he'd had enough of war. Shortly after Roosevelt led a charge by the Rough Riders on San Juan Hill, becoming an instant national hero, Remington sailed home on a hospital ship, tired and ill.

He recovered his health quickly and regained the weight he had lost also, soon weighing 295 pounds (134 kg). But he remained sick of war. Turning down requests to write and sketch his experiences in the war, Remington quickly began to sculpt again, always on western subjects. Soon he had completed his fourth model called *The Triumph*, while also writing short fiction for *Harper's Monthly*. Unknown to him, *Harper's* was having financial troubles and soon could no longer pay him the fees he now charged.

Remington switched to *Collier's Weekly*, although he refused to paint, write, or sketch anything about the war. He made one exception when Roosevelt asked him to paint *Charge of the Rough Riders at San Juan Hill* for *Scribner's Magazine*. The painting increased Roosevelt's popularity and promoted his political career. He was elected governor of New York State and then vice president of the United States.

In October 1901, Remington was forty years old. The month before, his friend, Vice President Theodore Roosevelt, at the age of forty-two, became the youngest president of the United States in history. President McKinley had been shot on September 6 and died eight days later.

Now Remington wanted to be known as a serious writer as well as a serious painter and began to write a long novel. It was not as easy as he'd expected and he agonized over it for one long summer at his vacation home. *The Virginian* by Owen

Charge of the Rough Riders at San Juan Hill,
commissioned by Scribner's Magazine *to illustrate*
Theodore Roosevelt's article on "The Cavalry at
Santiago," published in April 1899.

Wister had recently been published, becoming an instant best seller. Remington felt that his book, *John Ermine*, would be as popular, but it never succeeded with the critics or the public. Yet critics were amazed that an artist of Remington's talent could write as well as he did.

In 1903, Remington signed a contract with *Collier's* to paint twelve pictures in color each year for four years. For the first time, he was not to illustrate someone else's story or suggestions by the editor. He could choose his own ideas.

This contract could not have come at a better time. For many months, he had been working to alter his style of exacting realism and paint in the more popular Impressionist style that had become internationally popular with critics and public alike. Now the *Collier's* paintings gave him the chance to show how he had developed in this new style.

Remington's career continued to soar. On March 18, 1905, *Collier's* devoted its entire issue to him and his art. In that same year, he was commissioned by the Fairmount Park Art Association of Philadelphia to sculpt a cowboy on a horse for permanent outdoor display. It proved to be a difficult task, and three years would pass before it was completed and dedicated.

Yet, Remington continued to have doubts about his talent. Once, a beginning illustrator, Charles Shepard Chapman, came to ask for advice. Remington spent most of a weekend with him, using his own work to convey his thoughts and doubts and frustrations to the young man.

His frustrations involved his work on night scenes and landscapes that did not satisfy him. Suddenly, picking up a group of his own sketches, Remington began to throw them into the fire burning in his study fireplace. Chapman was horrified and so was Remington's wife, who was afraid that the fire would burn the house down. To calm her, Remington tossed the burning sketches out of a window into the snow. Later, Chapman carried away three of the ruined sketches as mementos of a day when he said he learned more about art than at any other time of his life.

In the years that followed, Remington turned out more work than most artists half his age who were in better physical condition. Although he traveled west several more times, the trips were no longer comfortable for him. His weight and lack of regular exercise made long horseback rides and rugged outdoor life on the trail intolerable.

But he was feeling more confident about his artistic ability. He confided to his diary that he had

*In 1900, Remington bought Ingleneuk Island in
Chippewa Bay, near his boyhood home in Ogdensburg,
New York. It was a summer retreat that gave him time
and space for serious painting.*

A Figure of The Night, *is dated 1908, a period when Remington was perfecting his technique of painting moonlight and shadows.*

now discovered "for the first time how to do the silver sheen of moonlight." He had worked for many years to accomplish this.

On January 25, 1908, Remington started another fire, outdoors this time, and burned sixteen more paintings. To him, this act signified the end of his being only an illustrator. Of course he could never completely rid himself of these paintings. They had been published, and many prints had been made, which were now hanging in homes throughout the nation. But he felt he had arrived at a point in his life where he could "paint running horses so you would feel the details and not see them." He and art critics agreed that he had become one of the top Impressionists in the country.

In early 1909, he attended a breakfast honoring his friend President Roosevelt and saw many of his friends from his westering days. Meanwhile, his wife had been working closely with an architect on their new home in Ridgefield, Connecticut. When they moved in on May 17, he found his studio decorated exactly as it had been at Endion, with all the western artifacts that he had bought or been given over the years. Placed in front of his easel was the rocking chair in which he always sat to paint.

He continued to paint throughout the summer and fall, despite a "constant bellyache." In late

Remington sculpting The Buffalo Horse *at the end of 1907. It is realistic action in bronze.*

December, doctors were called in and quickly decided to operate on Remington on the kitchen table at home. They discovered that his appendix had burst and an infection had spread throughout his body. He died on December 26, 1909, at the age of forty-eight, and was buried in his hometown of Canton, New York.

President Roosevelt spoke words of eulogy about his old friend. He said, "The soldier, the cowboy and rancher, the Indian, the horses and the cattle of the plains, will live in his pictures and bronzes . . . for all time."

When Frederic Remington was born in 1861, eleven states had seceded from the Union. Their attempt to retain slavery and states' rights within their borders failed, and the war ended in 1865. Slowly, the nation came together to bind up its wounds, then continue its westward expansion that had really begun in 1607 when Anglo-American pioneers made the first assault on the wilderness at Jamestown, Virginia.

Only the Great Plains remained to be settled at the end of the Civil War. Cattlemen transformed the Plains area into a giant pastureland until farmers arrived to fence fields and plow the soil. During Remington's lifetime, barbed-wire fences, wind-

Remington in a pensive mood before his fireplace in the studio of his new home in Ridgefield, Connecticut.

mills, railroads, and efficient farm machinery conquered the West until there was no more frontier.

Yet, interest in the West remained constant and became the subject of Remington's lifework. Even today, it continues to be celebrated in stories, songs, and art, largely influenced by the pen and brush of Frederic Remington, artist of the American West.

FOR FURTHER READING

Barker, Donna. *Frederic Remington*. Chicago: Childrens Press, 1977.

"Frederic Remington." *Cobblestone*. Peterborough, N.H.: Cobblestone Publishing, 1982.

Moore, Clyde B. *Frederic Remington, Young Artist*. Indianapolis: Bobbs-Merrill, 1971.

Peter, Adeline, and Ernest Lloyd Raboff. *Frederic Remington*. Garden City, N.Y.: Doubleday, 1973.

Raboff, Ernest Lloyd. *Frederic Remington*. New York: Harper & Row, 1988.

Stewart, John. *Frederic Remington, Artist of the Western Frontier*. New York: Lothrop, Lee & Shepard, 1971.

INDEX

Page numbers in *italics* indicate illustrations.

Elizabeth Van Steenwyk is the author of fifty books for young people and more than two hundred articles and short stories for children's and adult magazines. She is the recipient of the Helen Keating Ott award for her outstanding contribution to children's literature, presented by the Church and Synagogue Library Association for 1990. Her young adult biography *Ida B. Wells Barnett: Woman of Courage*, published in 1992 by Franklin Watts, was a NCSS/CBC Notable Children's Trade Book in the Field of Social Studies for 1992. Ms. Van Steenwyk lives with her husband in San Marino, California.